FORTUNE COOKIES

Small secrets on how to make a fortune

Dr. Roger D. Smith

Author of *Advice written on the back of a business card*
and *Texts 2 Teens*

Modelbenders Press

Fortune Cookies: Small secrets on how to make a fortune.

Copyright 2010 by Roger Smith. All rights reserved. No part of this book may be reproduced or transmitted in any form or by any means, electronic or mechanical, including photocopying, recording, or by any information storage and retrieval system, without written permission from the author. For information please forward your inquiries to Modelbenders Press, P.O. Box 781692, Orlando, Florida 32878.

Modelbenders Press books may be purchased for business and promotional use or for special sales. For information please contact the publisher.

Visit our web site at www.modelbenders.com

PRINTED IN THE UNITED STATES OF AMERICA

Designed by Adina Cucicov at Flamingo Designs

The Library of Congress has cataloged the paperback edition as follows:

Smith, Roger
    Fortune Cookies: Small secrets on how to make a fortune.
    Roger Smith—1st ed.
    1. Career—Management   2. Businesspeople—Conduct of Life   3. Financial Advice   4. Business Principles
    5. Self-Help: Personal Growth   Success
    I. Roger Smith   II. Title

ISBN-13: 978-0-9823040-9-9
ISBN-10: 0-9823040-9-9

Table of Contents

Fortune Cookies 3

Chapter 1: Actions 5

Chapter 2: Attitude 31

Chapter 3: Education 73

Chapter 4: Investing 93

Chapter 5: Money 109

Chapter 6: Principles 127

Chapter 7: Work 143

Fortune Cookies

Millions of Americans look forward to the end of a good Chinese dinner specifically because it is an opportunity to break open a fortune cookie and see what sage advice lies inside. Even though the message may be silly, vague, or random we never seem to tire of the ritual. In our enthusiasm for it we have even created a number of superstitions around how to open the cookie, whether to eat it or not, and whether it can be read aloud. We love to get advice and we are eager to do anything to help make it come true.

This book contains over 100 fortunes that specifically speak to your ability to make a fortune in your life. Each page has an original piece of advice provided by a world leader, successful business person, or philosopher.

History of the Fortune Cookie

The little fortune cookie has been part of American dining for over 100 years. Even though we enjoy them at Chinese restaurants, the original cookie actually was created in Kyoto, Japan. The Japanese preferred their cookies seasoned with sesame and miso, rather than the vanilla and butter flavor that we like in America. Slips of paper with words of wisdom and good luck were called "omikuji" and were distributed to worshipers

FORTUNE COOKIES

Small secrets on how to make a fortune

at Japanese temples. These were later inserted into the crevice of the uniquely shaped cookie and served with meals.

Until World War II, the American fortune cookie was manufactured and distributed by Japanese companies in America. Some of their most enthusiastic customers were the Chinese restaurants that were becoming popular in California. But with the internment of 100,000 Japanese-American civilians during the war, the manufacture and distribution of the cookie shifted to Chinese companies. As a result, most people believe that the cookies came to America from China rather than Japan.

It is not clear who the first person was to introduce the cookie in America. The three leading contendors are Makoto Hagiwara at his Golden Gate Japanese Tea Garden in San Francisco (1890); David Jung at his Hong Kong Noodle Company in Los Angeles (1918); and Seiichi Kito at Fugetsu-do of Little Tokyo in Los Angeles.

Today we consume over 3 billion fortune cookies every year. The advice in this book is a drop in a huge bucket, but this advice is worth a fortune.

Chapter 1

ACTIONS

FORTUNE COOKIES

Small secrets on how to make a fortune

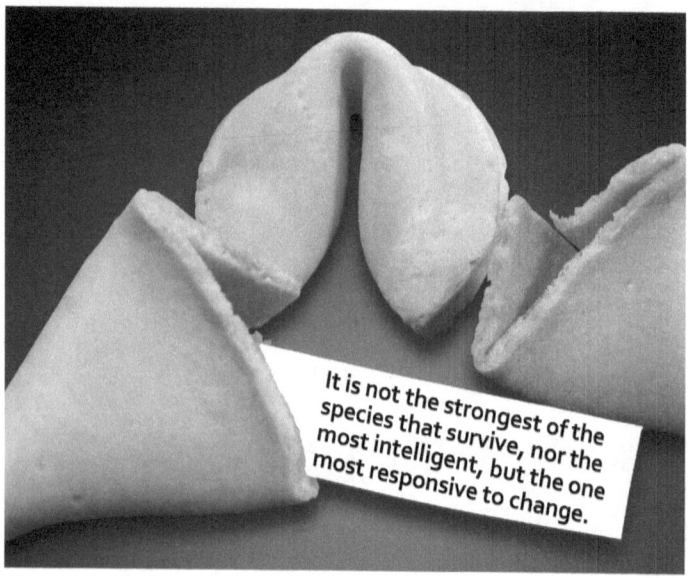

It is not the strongest of the species that survive, nor the most intelligent, but the one most responsive to change.

Charles Darwin
Scientist

FORTUNE COOKIES

Small secrets on how to make a fortune

Do what you do so well that they will want to see it again and bring their friends.

Walt Disney
Founder, Walt Disney Company

FORTUNE COOKIES

Small secrets on how to make a fortune

Work all of the time that you work.

Brian Tracy
Business Consultant

FORTUNE COOKIES
Small secrets on how to make a fortune

Become the best at one specific thing or become very good at two things.

Scott Adams
Creator of the Dilbert Cartoon

FORTUNE COOKIES

Small secrets on how to make a fortune

FORTUNE COOKIES

Small secrets on how to make a fortune

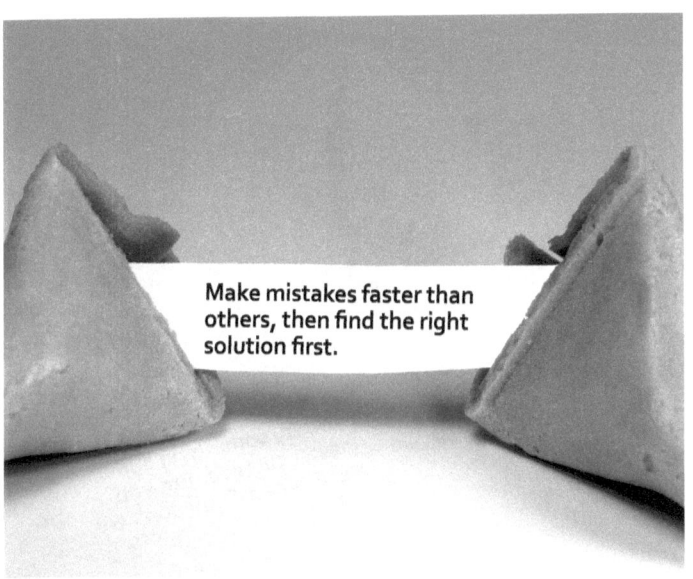

Make mistakes faster than others, then find the right solution first.

FORTUNE COOKIES

Small secrets on how to make a fortune

You may be disappointed if you try something and it doesn't succeed. But you are doomed if you don't try.

Robert H. Smith
Philanthropist

FORTUNE COOKIES

Small secrets on how to make a fortune

Felix Dennis
Founder, Maxim Magazine

FORTUNE COOKIES

Small secrets on how to make a fortune

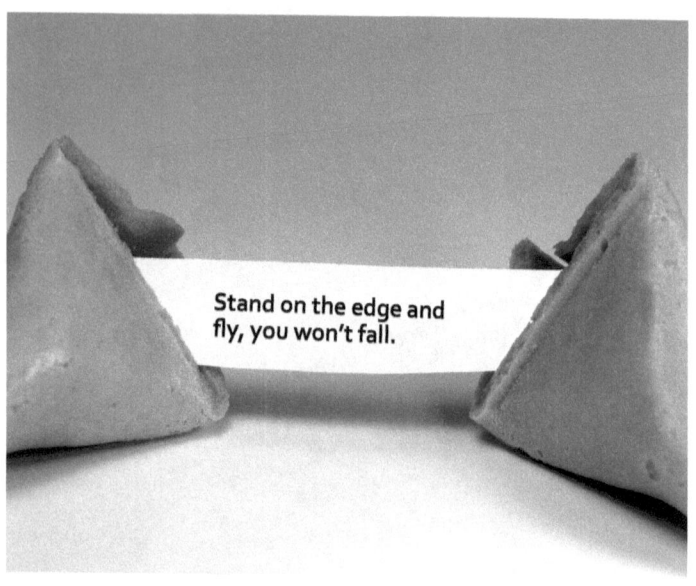

FORTUNE COOKIES

Small secrets on how to make a fortune

Keep your eye on the cheese. Go where the cheese goes.

FORTUNE COOKIES

Small secrets on how to make a fortune

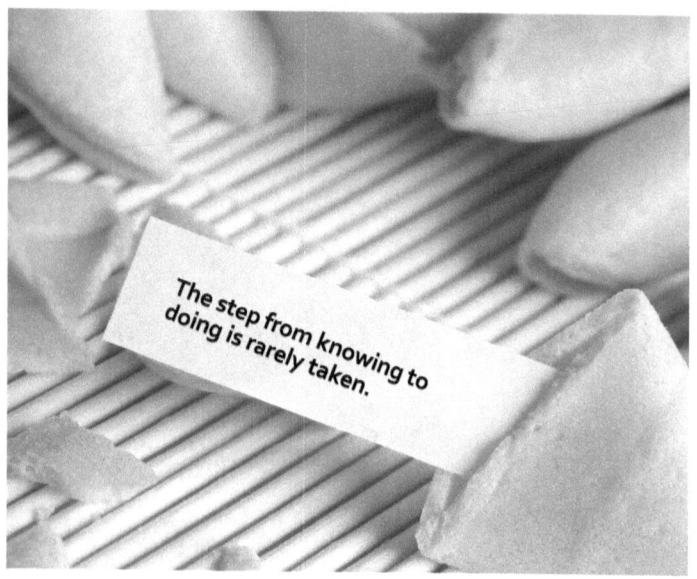

The step from knowing to doing is rarely taken.

Felix Dennis
Founder, Maxim Magazine

FORTUNE COOKIES

Small secrets on how to make a fortune

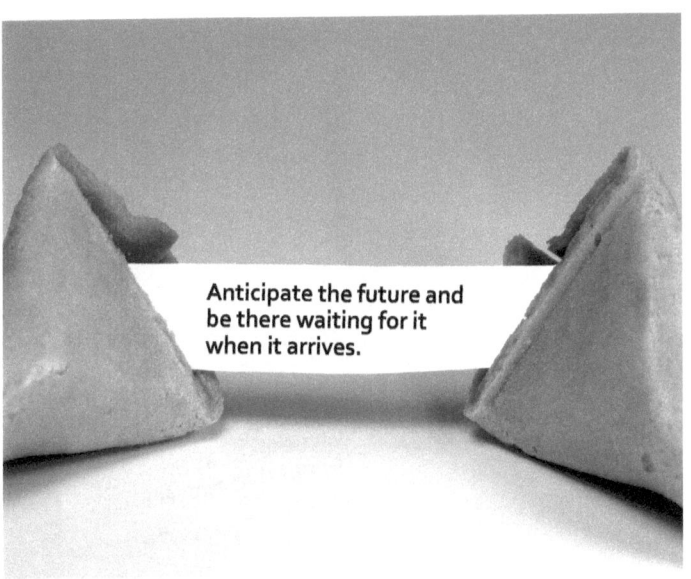

Anticipate the future and be there waiting for it when it arrives.

FORTUNE COOKIES

Small secrets on how to make a fortune

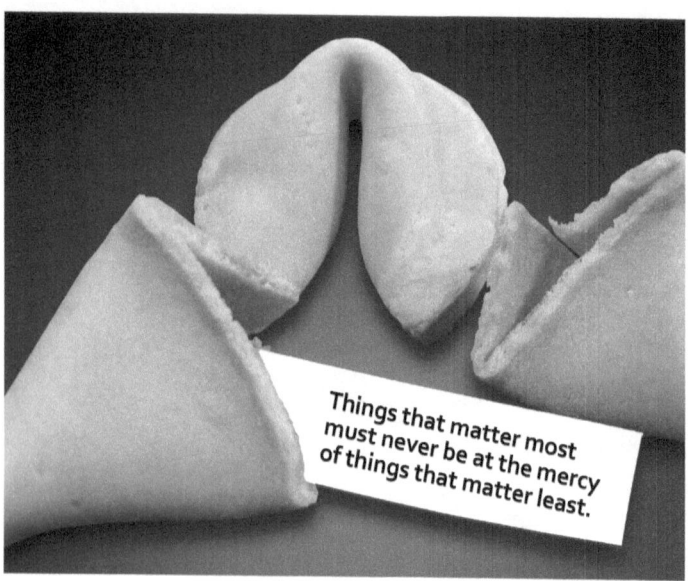

Things that matter most must never be at the mercy of things that matter least.

Goethe
Philosopher

FORTUNE COOKIES

Small secrets on how to make a fortune

If you do not use your abilities, you are stealing from yourself.

FORTUNE COOKIES
Small secrets on how to make a fortune

Failure is the line of least persistence.

Zig Ziglar
Author and Speaker

FORTUNE COOKIES

Small secrets on how to make a fortune

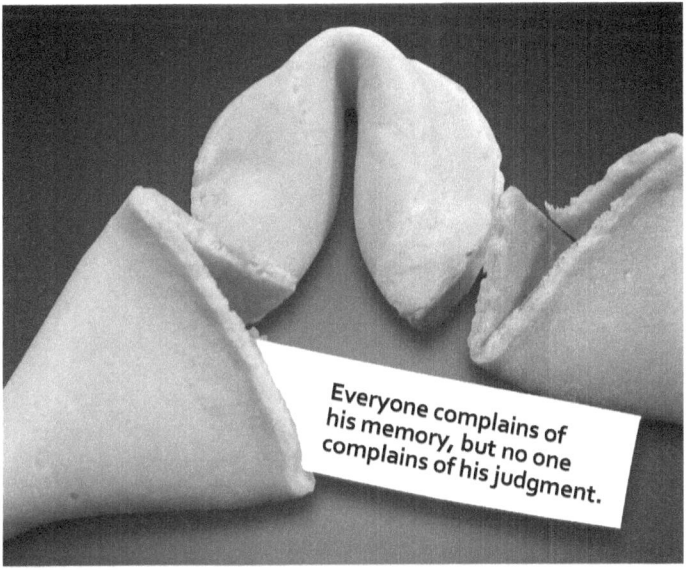

Everyone complains of his memory, but no one complains of his judgment.

Francois Duc de la Rochefoucauld

FORTUNE COOKIES
Small secrets on how to make a fortune

Ask for what you want. Don't assume the other person already knows.

Richard Carlson
Author

FORTUNE COOKIES

Small secrets on how to make a fortune

Luke 6:38

FORTUNE COOKIES

Small secrets on how to make a fortune

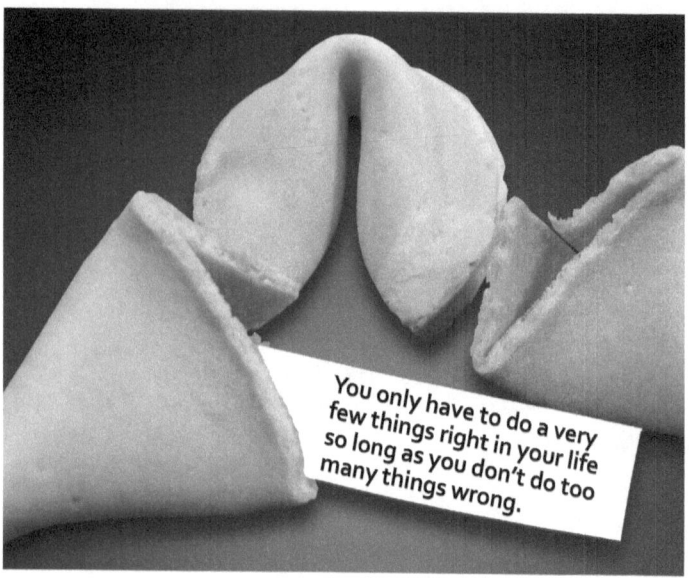

Warren Buffett
Investor

FORTUNE COOKIES

Small secrets on how to make a fortune

FORTUNE COOKIES

Small secrets on how to make a fortune

FORTUNE COOKIES

Small secrets on how to make a fortune

Plans are useless but planning is indispensible.

Dwight Eisenhower
President of the United States

FORTUNE COOKIES

Small secrets on how to make a fortune

FORTUNE COOKIES

Small secrets on how to make a fortune

Be willing to do it wrong before you get it right.

# Chapter 2

ATTITUDE

FORTUNE COOKIES
Small secrets on how to make a fortune

Bill Waite
Chairman and CTO,
Aegis Technologies Group

FORTUNE COOKIES

Small secrets on how to make a fortune

Stop talking like you are poor and ignorant.

FORTUNE COOKIES

Small secrets on how to make a fortune

You can make excuses,
or you can make money,
but you can't do both.

Richard Carlson
Author

FORTUNE COOKIES

Small secrets on how to make a fortune

FORTUNE COOKIES

Small secrets on how to make a fortune

The Seven Dwarfs

FORTUNE COOKIES

Small secrets on how to make a fortune

FORTUNE COOKIES

Small secrets on how to make a fortune

Respond to change, do not react to it.

FORTUNE COOKIES

Small secrets on how to make a fortune

FORTUNE COOKIES

Small secrets on how to make a fortune

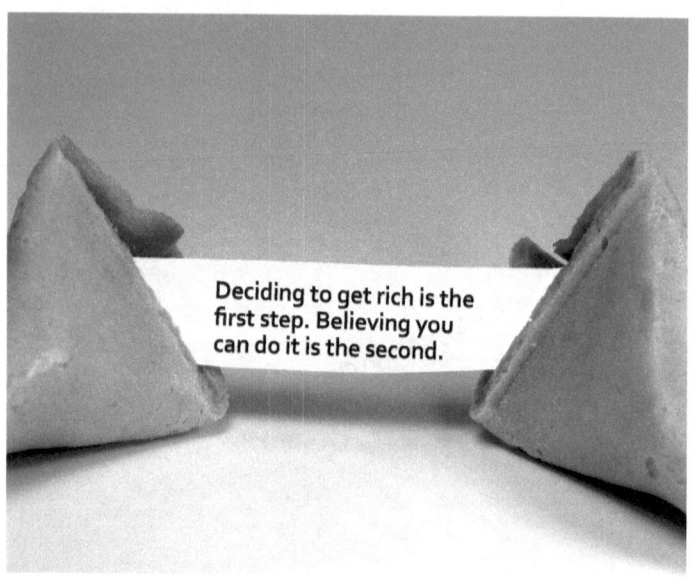

Deciding to get rich is the first step. Believing you can do it is the second.

FORTUNE COOKIES

Small secrets on how to make a fortune

I am the captain of my soul;
I am the master of my fate.

William Henley
British Poet

FORTUNE COOKIES

Small secrets on how to make a fortune

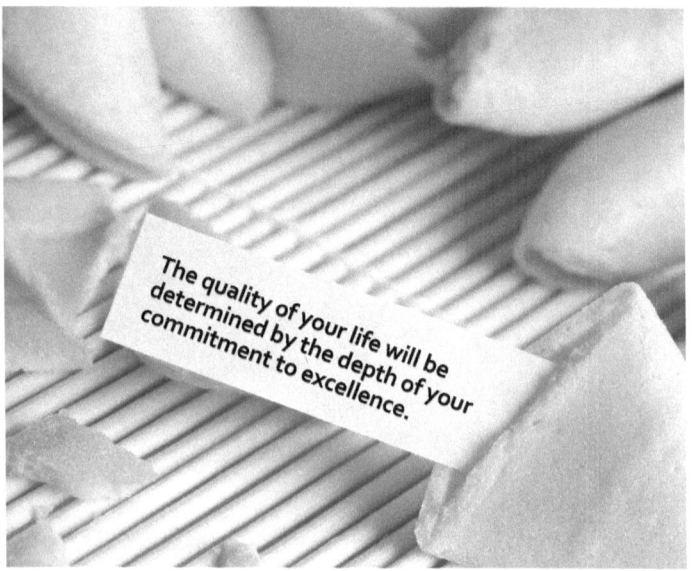

The quality of your life will be determined by the depth of your commitment to excellence.

Vince Lombardi
Football Coach

FORTUNE COOKIES

Small secrets on how to make a fortune

Fear of failing is the single biggest impediment to getting wealthy.

Felix Dennis
Founder, Maxim Magazine

FORTUNE COOKIES

Small secrets on how to make a fortune

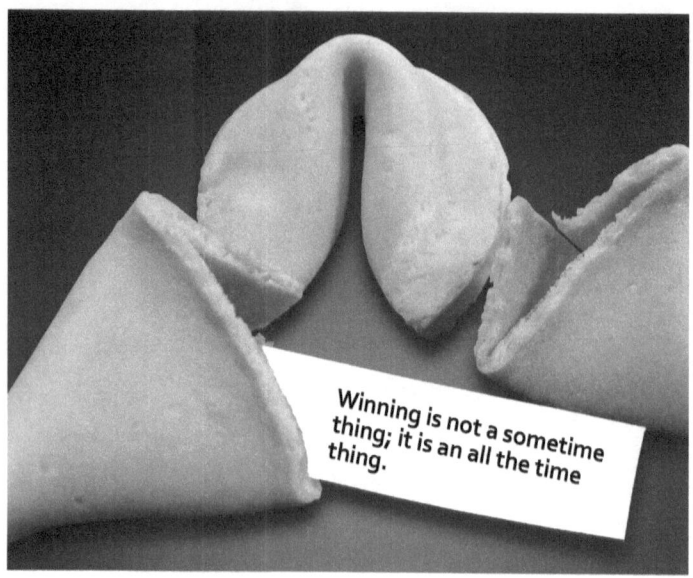

Winning is not a sometime thing; it is an all the time thing.

Vince Lombardi
Football Coach

FORTUNE COOKIES
Small secrets on how to make a fortune

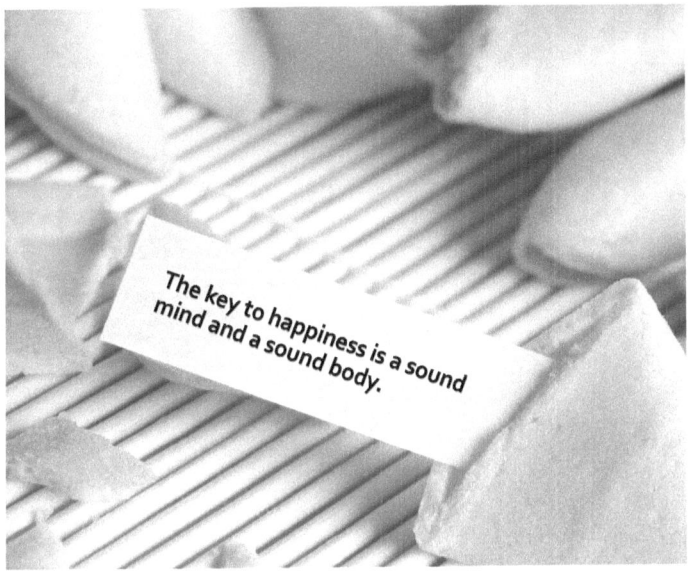

Theodore Roosevelt
President of the United States

FORTUNE COOKIES

Small secrets on how to make a fortune

Epictetus
Greek Philosopher

FORTUNE COOKIES

Small secrets on how to make a fortune

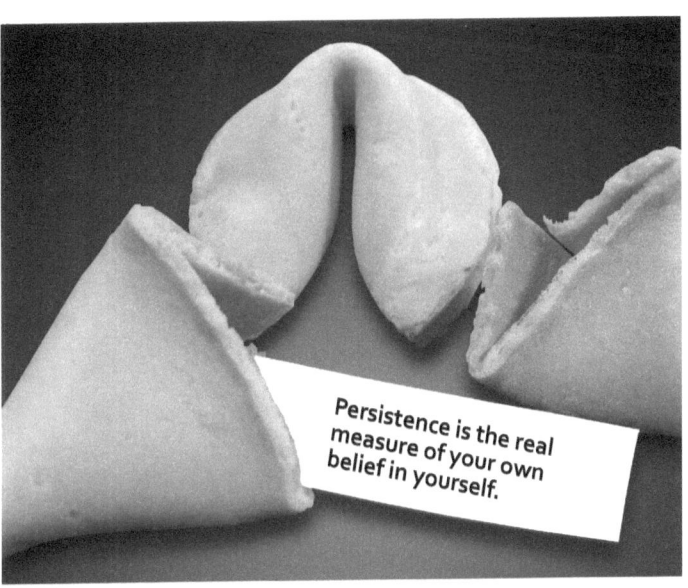

Persistence is the real measure of your own belief in yourself.

FORTUNE COOKIES

Small secrets on how to make a fortune

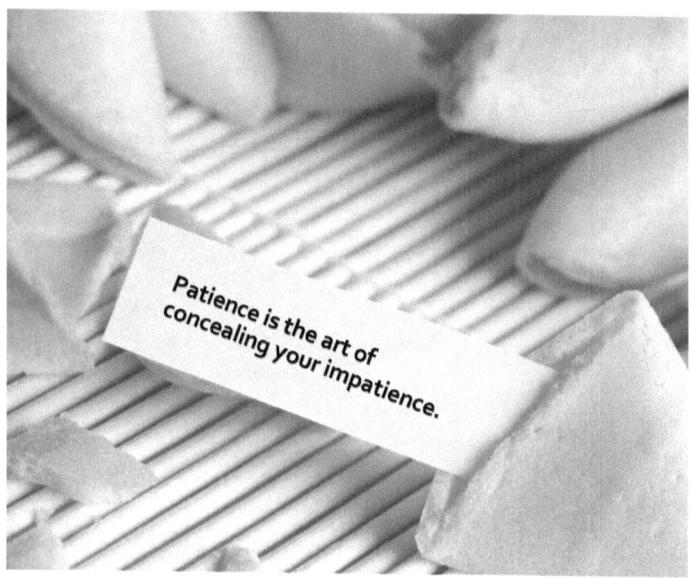

Patience is the art of concealing your impatience.

Guy Kawasaki
Apple Computer

FORTUNE COOKIES
Small secrets on how to make a fortune

Success isn't permanent, and failure isn't fatal.

Robert H. Smith
Philanthropist

FORTUNE COOKIES

Small secrets on how to make a fortune

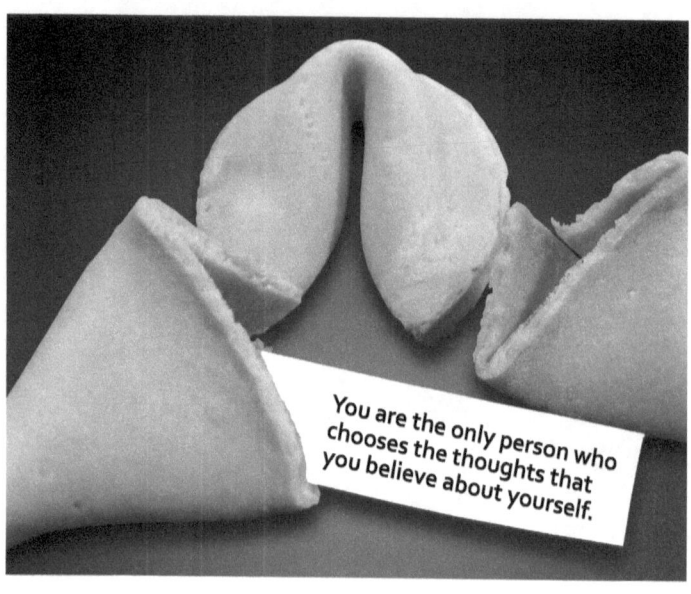

You are the only person who chooses the thoughts that you believe about yourself.

FORTUNE COOKIES

Small secrets on how to make a fortune

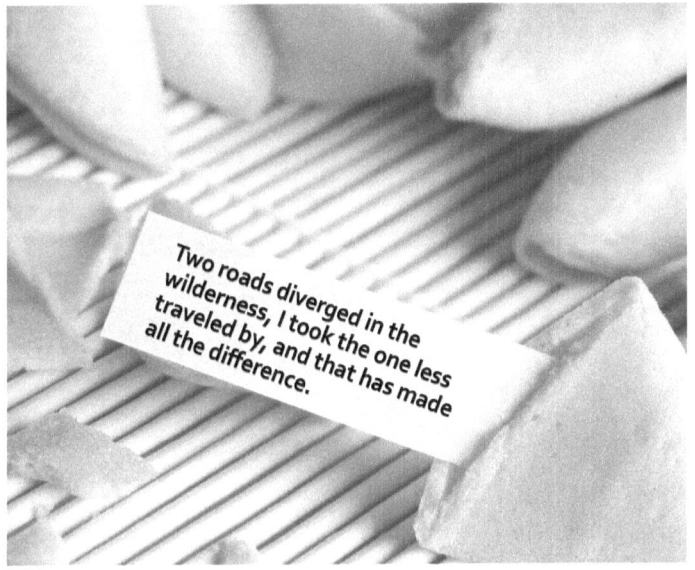

Robert Frost
Author

FORTUNE COOKIES

Small secrets on how to make a fortune

Focus on opportunities, not obstacles.

FORTUNE COOKIES

Small secrets on how to make a fortune

High expectations are the key to everything.

Robert H. Smith
Philanthropist

FORTUNE COOKIES

Small secrets on how to make a fortune

If you promote yourself, you promote your wealth.

FORTUNE COOKIES

Small secrets on how to make a fortune

Charge boldly and vocally at what you want.

FORTUNE COOKIES

Small secrets on how to make a fortune

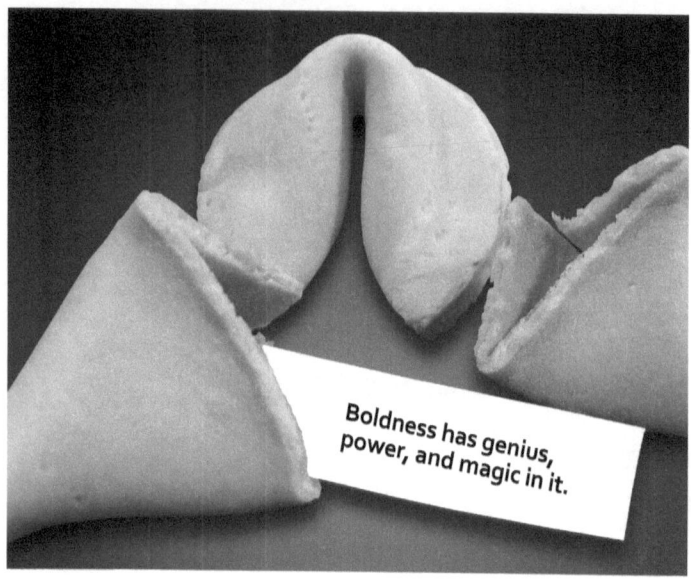

Boldness has genius, power, and magic in it.

Felix Dennis
Founder, Maxim Magazine

FORTUNE COOKIES
Small secrets on how to make a fortune

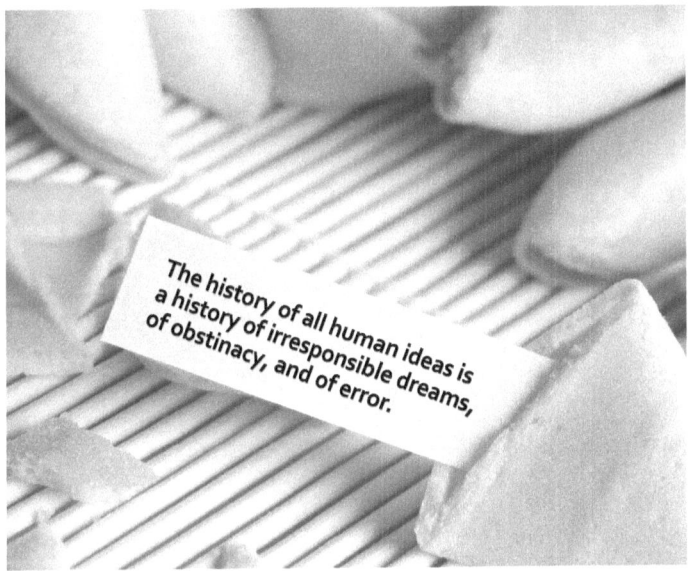

The history of all human ideas is a history of irresponsible dreams, of obstinacy, and of error.

Karl Popper
Sociologist

FORTUNE COOKIES

Small secrets on how to make a fortune

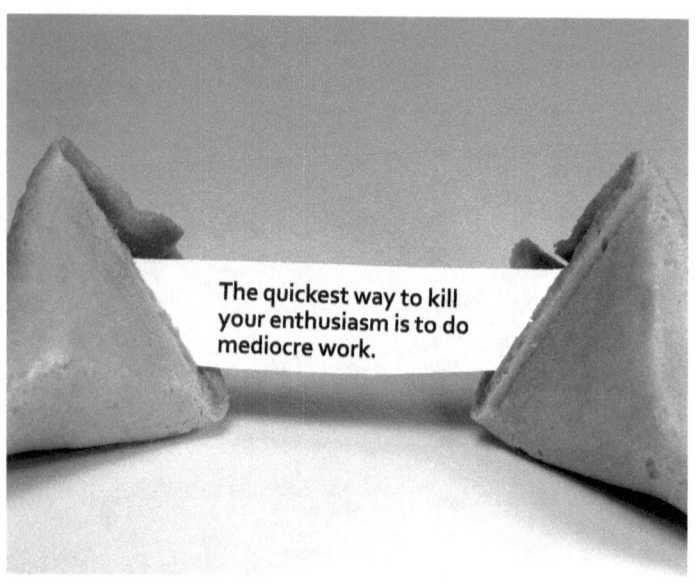

FORTUNE COOKIES

Small secrets on how to make a fortune

Worry is a misuse of the imagination.

Zig Ziglar
Author and Speaker

FORTUNE COOKIES

Small secrets on how to make a fortune

Seneca
Roman Philosopher

FORTUNE COOKIES
Small secrets on how to make a fortune

Marcus Aurelius
Roman Emperor

FORTUNE COOKIES

Small secrets on how to make a fortune

Team spirit is the glue that binds losers together.

Felix Dennis
Founder, Maxim Magazine

FORTUNE COOKIES

Small secrets on how to make a fortune

If the fear of losing stops you from investing, then you have already lost.

FORTUNE COOKIES

Small secrets on how to make a fortune

Listen twice as much as you talk.

FORTUNE COOKIES

Small secrets on how to make a fortune

Build your confidence through harder successes.

FORTUNE COOKIES

Small secrets on how to make a fortune

Don't panic—and don't show it when you do.

Richard Carlson
Author

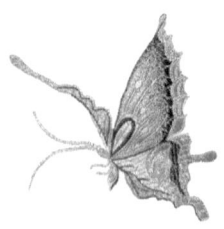

FORTUNE COOKIES

Small secrets on how to make a fortune

FORTUNE COOKIES
Small secrets on how to make a fortune

Franklin Roosevelt
President of the United States

FORTUNE COOKIES

Small secrets on how to make a fortune

You are not part of a team, though you might have to pretend that you are.

Felix Dennis
Founder, Maxim Magazine

FORTUNE COOKIES

Small secrets on how to make a fortune

Richard Carlson
Author

FORTUNE COOKIES

Small secrets on how to make a fortune

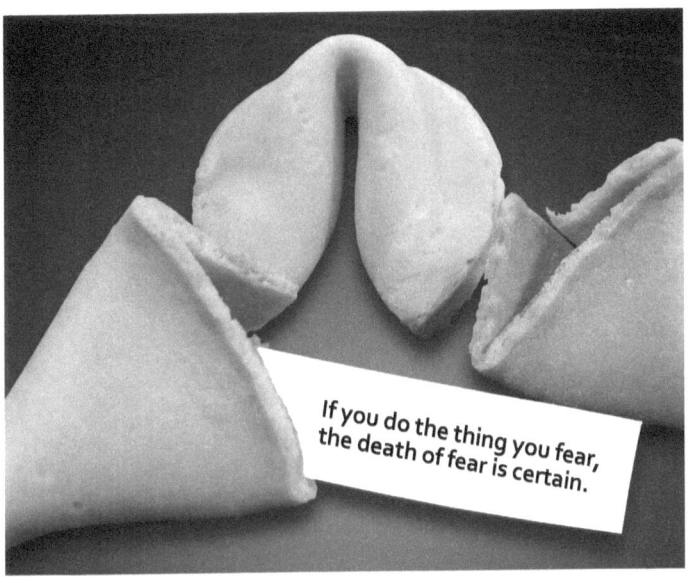

If you do the thing you fear, the death of fear is certain.

Ralph Waldo Emerson
Author

FORTUNE COOKIES

Small secrets on how to make a fortune

Have an unshakable belief that it can be done and you are the one to do it.

Felix Dennis
Founder, Maxim Magazine

Chapter 3

EDUCATION

FORTUNE COOKIES

Small secrets on how to make a fortune

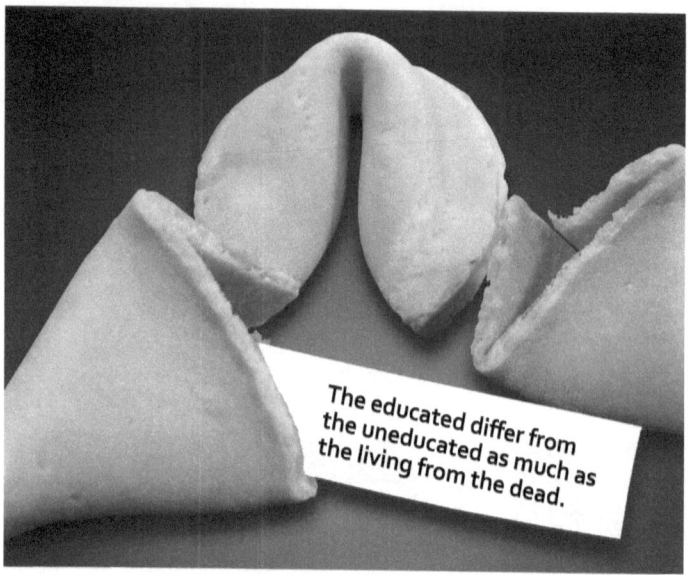

The educated differ from the uneducated as much as the living from the dead.

Aristotle
Philosopher

FORTUNE COOKIES

Small secrets on how to make a fortune

Buy knowledge and expertise.

FORTUNE COOKIES

Small secrets on how to make a fortune

Stupidity makes you a victim.

FORTUNE COOKIES

Small secrets on how to make a fortune

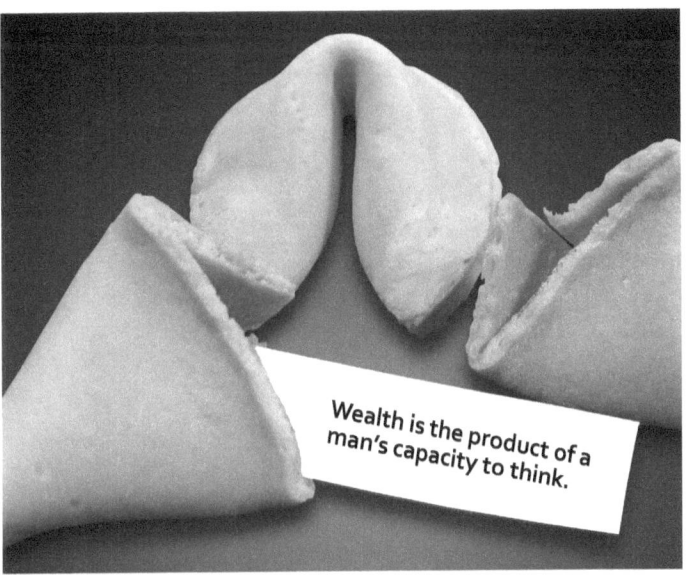

Wealth is the product of a man's capacity to think.

Ayn Rand
Philosopher

FORTUNE COOKIES

Small secrets on how to make a fortune

Your money only grows when you grow.

FORTUNE COOKIES

Small secrets on how to make a fortune

It takes more homework to earn money than it does to earn grades.

FORTUNE COOKIES

Small secrets on how to make a fortune

Success is a lousy teacher. It seduces smart people into thinking they can't lose.

Bill Gates
Microsoft

FORTUNE COOKIES

Small secrets on how to make a fortune

Anyone not busy learning is busy dying.

Felix Dennis
Founder, Maxim Magazine

FORTUNE COOKIES

Small secrets on how to make a fortune

FORTUNE COOKIES

Small secrets on how to make a fortune

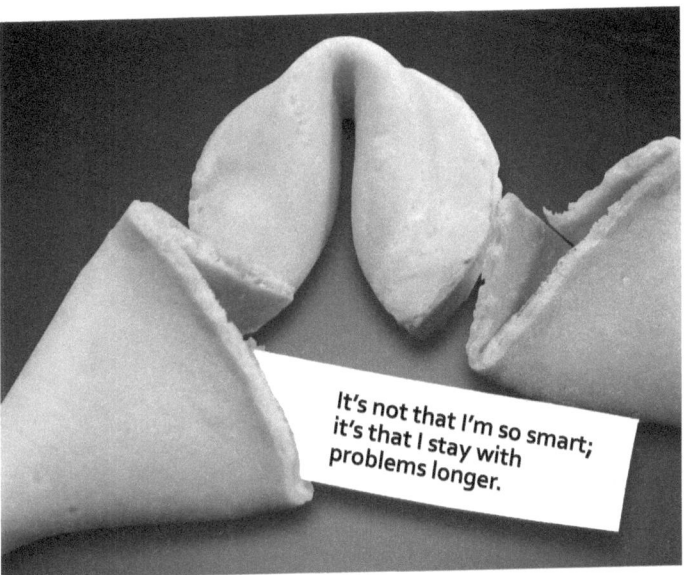

It's not that I'm so smart; it's that I stay with problems longer.

Albert Einstein
Scientist

FORTUNE COOKIES
Small secrets on how to make a fortune

Pay attention to silence. That is when a lot is being said.

John Heider
Author

FORTUNE COOKIES

Small secrets on how to make a fortune

Richard Carlson
Author

FORTUNE COOKIES

Small secrets on how to make a fortune

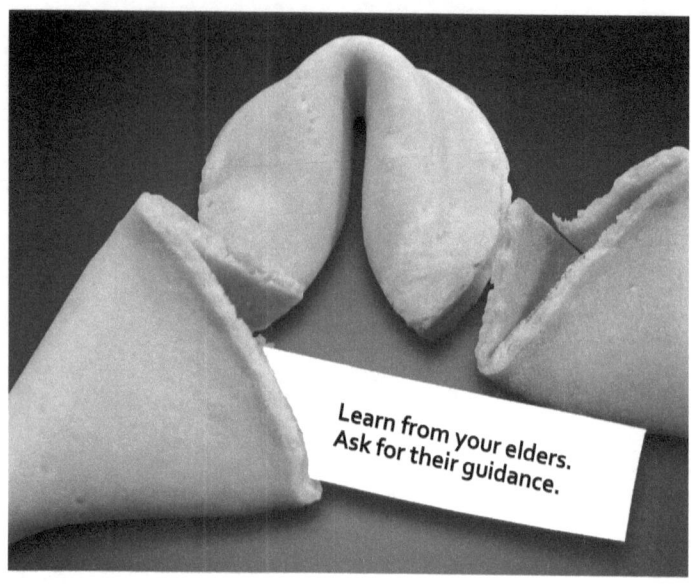

Learn from your elders. Ask for their guidance.

FORTUNE COOKIES

Small secrets on how to make a fortune

Accept advice and think about it before you speak.

FORTUNE COOKIES
Small secrets on how to make a fortune

Brian Tracy
Author

FORTUNE COOKIES

Small secrets on how to make a fortune

If you want to improve yourself, try silent contemplation.

John Heider
Author

FORTUNE COOKIES

Small secrets on how to make a fortune

Reading is to the mind what exercise is to the body.

FORTUNE COOKIES
Small secrets on how to make a fortune

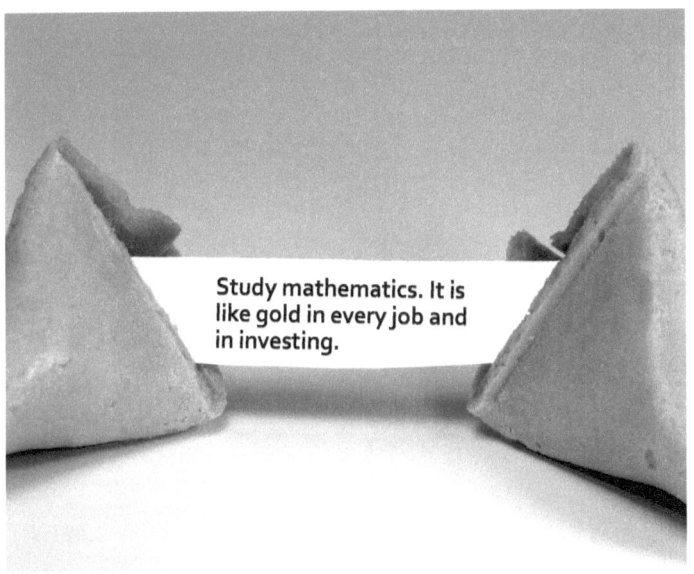

Study mathematics. It is like gold in every job and in investing.

Ralph Huntsinger
Professor

Chapter 4

INVESTING

FORTUNE COOKIES

Small secrets on how to make a fortune

FORTUNE COOKIES

Small secrets on how to make a fortune

Buy everything when it is on sale. Never pay full price.

FORTUNE COOKIES

Small secrets on how to make a fortune

Escape the madness of the crowds.

FORTUNE COOKIES

Small secrets on how to make a fortune

FORTUNE COOKIES

Small secrets on how to make a fortune

FORTUNE COOKIES

Small secrets on how to make a fortune

There is always a new South Sea scam.

FORTUNE COOKIES

Small secrets on how to make a fortune

"Get rich quick" is just for the guy selling it.

FORTUNE COOKIES
Small secrets on how to make a fortune

Rule No.1: Never lose money.
Rule No.2: Never forget rule No.1.

Warren Buffett
Investor

FORTUNE COOKIES

Small secrets on how to make a fortune

Warren Buffett
Investor

FORTUNE COOKIES
Small secrets on how to make a fortune

Be fearful when others are greedy and greedy when others are fearful.

Warren Buffett
Investor

FORTUNE COOKIES
Small secrets on how to make a fortune

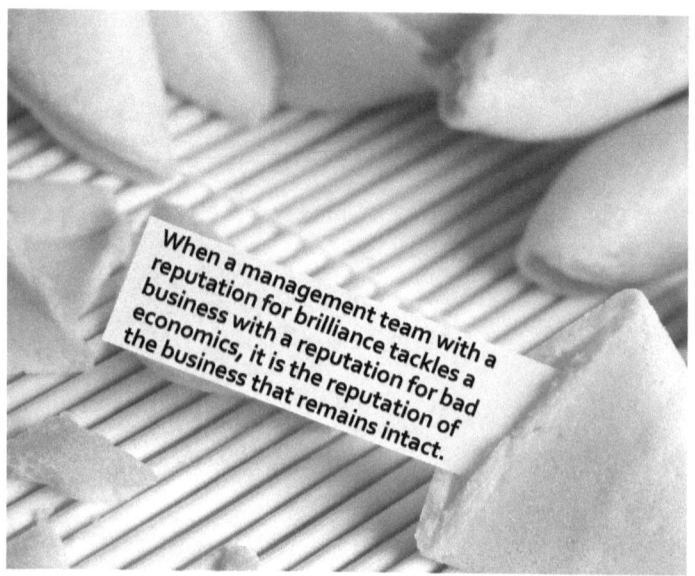

When a management team with a reputation for brilliance tackles a business with a reputation for bad economics, it is the reputation of the business that remains intact.

Warren Buffett
Investor

FORTUNE COOKIES

Small secrets on how to make a fortune

Pay yourself first.

FORTUNE COOKIES

Small secrets on how to make a fortune

Keep a part of every dollar that you earn.

FORTUNE COOKIES

Small secrets on how to make a fortune

FORTUNE COOKIES

Small secrets on how to make a fortune

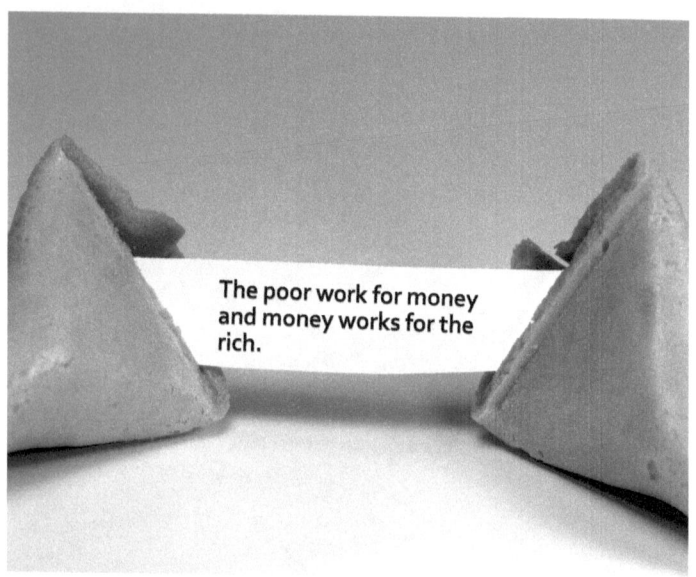

Brian Tracy
Business Consultant

Chapter 5

MONEY

FORTUNE COOKIES

Small secrets on how to make a fortune

FORTUNE COOKIES

Small secrets on how to make a fortune

Live, but well within your means.

FORTUNE COOKIES

Small secrets on how to make a fortune

Money is a number so wealth requires some mathematics.

FORTUNE COOKIES

Small secrets on how to make a fortune

FORTUNE COOKIES

Small secrets on how to make a fortune

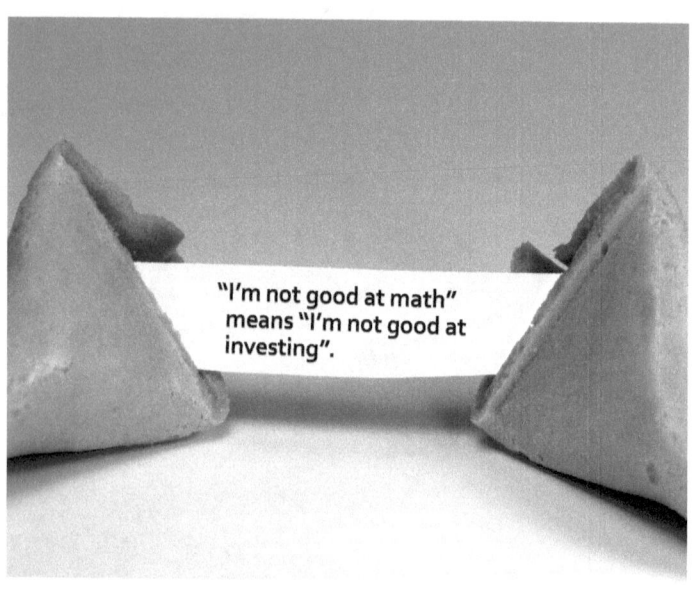

FORTUNE COOKIES

Small secrets on how to make a fortune

How much do you think you deserve? That is what you will get.

FORTUNE COOKIES

Small secrets on how to make a fortune

FORTUNE COOKIES

Small secrets on how to make a fortune

If you get a bonus, your savings gets a bonus.

FORTUNE COOKIES

Small secrets on how to make a fortune

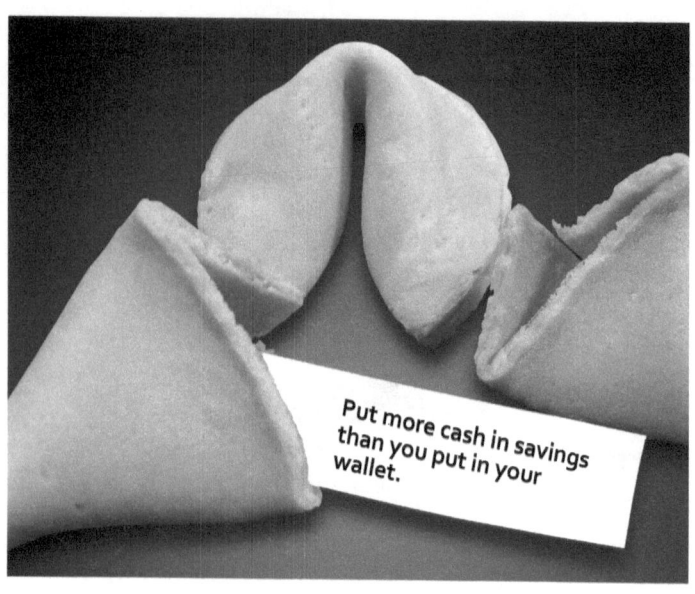

Put more cash in savings than you put in your wallet.

FORTUNE COOKIES

Small secrets on how to make a fortune

Buy a soda from yourself every day.

FORTUNE COOKIES

Small secrets on how to make a fortune

FORTUNE COOKIES

Small secrets on how to make a fortune

You can't make money where there is no money.

FORTUNE COOKIES

Small secrets on how to make a fortune

FORTUNE COOKIES

Small secrets on how to make a fortune

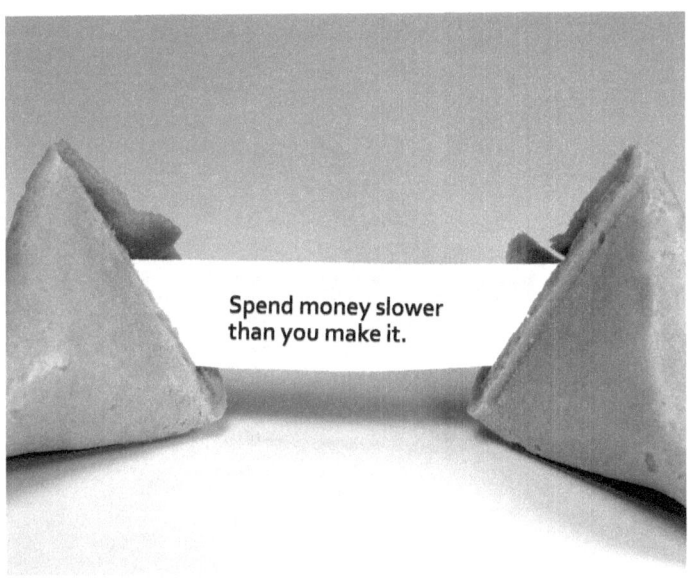

Spend money slower than you make it.

FORTUNE COOKIES

Small secrets on how to make a fortune

It is difficult for an empty sack to stand upright.

Benjamin Franklin
Inventor, Publisher, Statesman

FORTUNE COOKIES

Small secrets on how to make a fortune

Fortune is a matter of cause and effect. What are you causing to happen?

Chapter 6

PRINCIPLES

FORTUNE COOKIES

Small secrets on how to make a fortune

FORTUNE COOKIES

Small secrets on how to make a fortune

Follow the rules, until you're ready not to.

Jim Stogsdill
CTO, Mission Systems, Accenture

FORTUNE COOKIES

Small secrets on how to make a fortune

Guy Kawasaki
Apple Inc.

FORTUNE COOKIES

Small secrets on how to make a fortune

FORTUNE COOKIES

Small secrets on how to make a fortune

FORTUNE COOKIES

Small secrets on how to make a fortune

Create a great impression on the people you meet, not just a good one.

Richard Carlson
Author

FORTUNE COOKIES

Small secrets on how to make a fortune

FORTUNE COOKIES
Small secrets on how to make a fortune

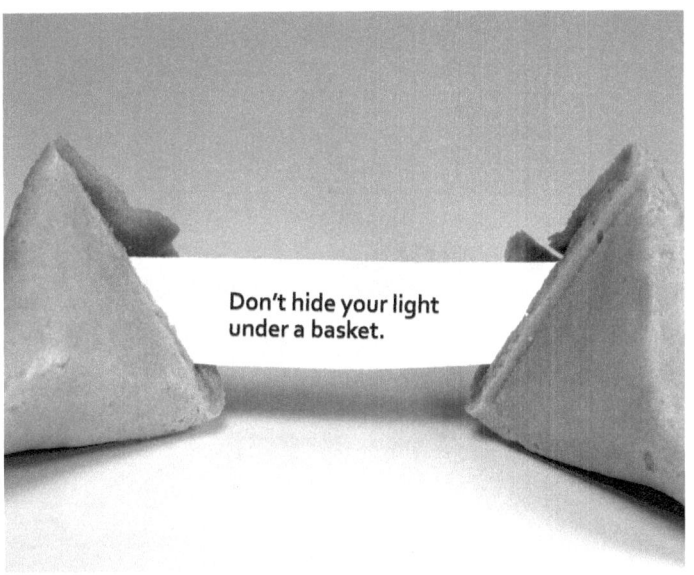

Matthew 5:15

FORTUNE COOKIES

Small secrets on how to make a fortune

FORTUNE COOKIES

Small secrets on how to make a fortune

FORTUNE COOKIES

Small secrets on how to make a fortune

Dream big dreams; only big dreams have the power to move men's souls.

Marcus Aurelius
Roman Emperor

FORTUNE COOKIES

Small secrets on how to make a fortune

FORTUNE COOKIES

Small secrets on how to make a fortune

Imagination is more important than knowledge.

Albert Einstein
Scientist

FORTUNE COOKIES

Small secrets on how to make a fortune

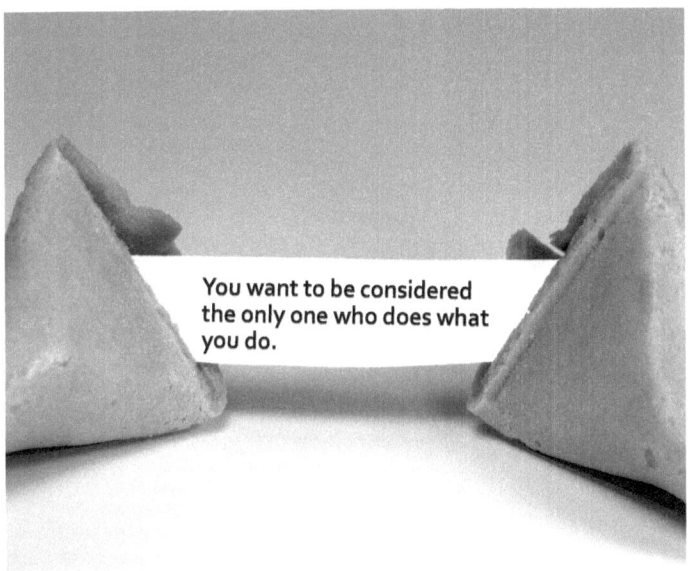

You want to be considered the only one who does what you do.

Jerry Garcia
Musician

Chapter 7

WORK

FORTUNE COOKIES

Small secrets on how to make a fortune

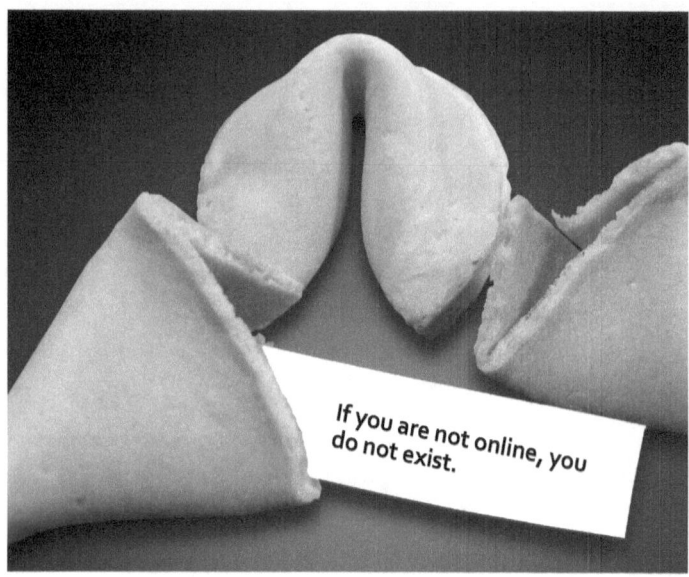

Irantzu Gonzalez
Manager, BMW Group

FORTUNE COOKIES
Small secrets on how to make a fortune

Find partners for all of your endeavors.

Richard Carlson
Author

FORTUNE COOKIES

Small secrets on how to make a fortune

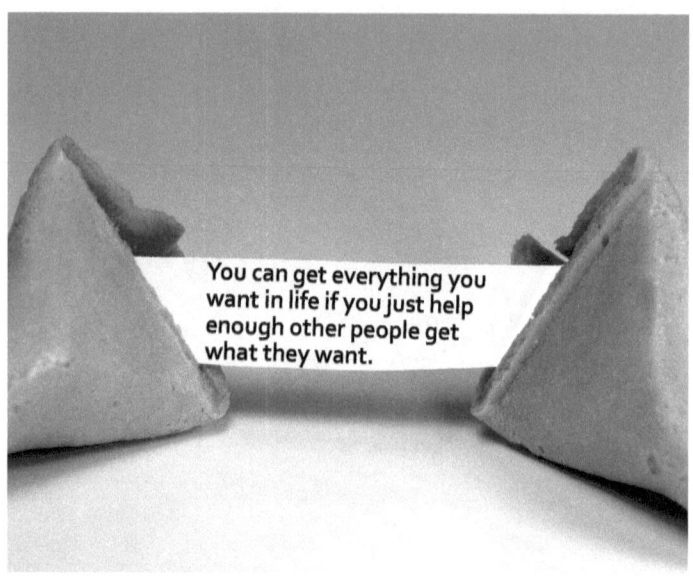

Zig Ziglar
Author

FORTUNE COOKIES
Small secrets on how to make a fortune

The hungry dog hunts best.

Norman Augustine
CEO, Lockheed Martin

FORTUNE COOKIES

Small secrets on how to make a fortune

Richard Carlson
Author

FORTUNE COOKIES

Small secrets on how to make a fortune

FORTUNE COOKIES

Small secrets on how to make a fortune

FORTUNE COOKIES

Small secrets on how to make a fortune

James Thurber
Author

FORTUNE COOKIES

Small secrets on how to make a fortune

Spend your time doing what is most valuable.

FORTUNE COOKIES
Small secrets on how to make a fortune

Calvin Coolidge
President of the United States

FORTUNE COOKIES
Small secrets on how to make a fortune

Guy Kawasaki
Apple Inc.

FORTUNE COOKIES

Small secrets on how to make a fortune

Do work that you think is cool. Others will think so too.

FORTUNE COOKIES
Small secrets on how to make a fortune

Pursue your passion and let it guide the choices you make every day.

Janet Weisenford
Fellow, icf International